14.50

FR. WATTS

69/10

D0124385

A New True Book

VENUS

By Dennis B. Fradin

CHILDRENS PRESS ®

CHICAGO

DR. THOMAS A. SWIFT ELEMENTARY SCHOOL
SCHOOL DISTRICT No. 34 (ABBOTSFORD)

Artist's drawing of Venus

American Museum of Natural History/PK208—40

Art—John Forsberg—14, 15

The Bettmann Archive—9, 10, 12, 19 (right), 23, 26, 28 (right top & bottom)

California Institute of Technology and Carnegie Institution of Washington—24 (right)

David Peterson—39 (both)

Field Museum of Natural History, Chicago/A77818C—4

NASA—2, 6, 7, 13, 30, 33, 34 (both), 37, 43 (left), 45

NASA-JET PROPULSION LAB—Cover, 17, 21

James Oberg—28 (left), 43 (right)

AP/Wide World Photos—42

Yerkes Observatory Photograph—11, 19 (left), 24 (left)

COVER: Mariner 10 photograph of Venus

For Matt and Katy Wirman

Library of Congress Cataloging-in-Publication Data

Fradin, Dennis B.
  Venus/by Dennis B. Fradin.
    p.   cm.—(A New true book)
  Includes index.
  Summary: Describes the characteristics of the second closest planet to the sun.
  ISBN 0-516-01168-5
  1. Venus (Planet)—Juvenile literature. [1. Venus (Planet) 2. Planets] I. Title. II. Series.
QB621.F73 1989   88-39121
523.4'2—dc19   CIP
                                          AC

Copyright © 1989 by Childrens Press®, Inc.
All rights reserved. Published simultaneously in Canada.
Printed in the United States of America.
1 2 3 4 5 6 7 8 9 10 R 98 97 96 95 94 93 92 91 90 89

TABLE OF CONTENTS

Ancient people worshiped the Sun and the other heavenly bodies.

VENUS AND ANCIENT PEOPLE

Stars last for billions of years. So when the ancient people looked up and saw the stars in the sky, they saw the same stars that we see today.

The ancients also saw seven heavenly bodies that looked different than the stars. The biggest and brightest object they saw

Solar eruption photographed by the *Skylab*

was the Sun. The second
largest object they saw
was the moon. It looked
the same size as the Sun,
but it wasn't as bright.

There also were five
starlike objects that didn't
act like stars. They didn't

Apollo 11 photographed the moon.

twinkle as stars do. They moved differently. These five objects were the planets Mercury, Venus, Mars, Jupiter, and Saturn.

Of the five objects the white planet, Venus, was by far the brightest. Except for the Sun and Moon, Venus is the brightest heavenly body seen from the Earth. Venus can even be seen in the daytime, if you know where to look.

The ancient people did not know what the planets were. They thought they were gods and goddesses. Because Venus was so beautiful, many people thought it was a goddess.

The Babylonians (people who lived in what is now Iraq) called Venus *Ishtar*.

The Babylonians believed Ishtar was the mother of all gods.

She was thought to be the mother of the gods. The Babylonians built temples to honor Ishtar. A Babylonian tablet showing observations of Venus dates back almost 4,000 years.

DR. THOMAS A. SWIFT ELEMENTARY SCHOOL SCHOOL DISTRICT No. 34 (ABBOTSFORD)

Venus was the Roman goddess of love and beauty.

The Chinese called Venus *Tai-pe*, the Beautiful White One. The Egyptians called it *Bonou*, the Bird. The Romans named the planet *Venus*, after their goddess of love and beauty. We still call the planet by its Roman name.

VENUS IS PART OF THE SOLAR SYSTEM

Nicolaus Copernicus

Until the 1500s, people had many wrong ideas about the heavenly bodies. For example, they thought the Earth was the center of the universe. They thought that the moon, planets, and stars moved around the Earth. The Polish astronomer Nicolaus Copernicus (1473-1543) proved this wrong.

In the 1700s English astronomers at the Royal Observatory at Greenwich, England, used wooden telescopes to study the heavens.

The first telescopes were built in the early 1600s. Telescopes make distant objects look closer. They gave astronomers a better picture of the sky.

Star cloud in the constellation Sagittarius

The truth is that space
contains billions of stars.
Our Sun is a star, and just
an average-sized one. It
looks big and bright
because it is closer to the
Earth than the other stars.

Nine planets orbit the Sun. Mercury is the planet closest to the Sun. Venus is next. Our home planet, Earth, is third. Then come Mars, Jupiter, Saturn, Uranus, Neptune, and Pluto. The last three were discovered by scientists using telescopes.

The ancient people were right about the planets moving differently than the stars. This happens because the planets are orbiting the Sun. The planets don't twinkle because they don't make light as stars do. Planets are lit by the Sun. Earth's air plays fewer tricks with the planets' reflected light than it does with direct starlight.

Seven planets have *moons* orbiting them. The Earth has one moon. Saturn has more than 19 moons. Mercury and Venus are the only planets without moons.

Saturn is surrounded by rings and more than 19 moons.

The Sun, planets, and moons are the main objects in the *Solar System*. The Solar System can be pictured as a "family" of objects with the Sun in the center.

17

OBSERVING VENUS FROM THE EARTH

The time that a planet takes to orbit the Sun is its year. The Earth orbits the Sun in 365¼ days, so our year is 365¼ days long. The closer a planet is to the Sun, the shorter its year. Venus's year is 225 Earth-days—the time Venus takes to orbit the Sun. Astronomers figured that out even before there were telescopes.

Galileo (above) discovered that Venus (left),
reflecting light from the Sun goes through
phases, just like the Earth's moon.

The first telescopes of
the early 1600s showed
two surprises about Venus.
The Italian astronomer
Galileo (1564-1642)
learned that Venus passes
through *phases* like the
Moon. Sometimes it looks
like a thin crescent. Other

19

times it is half or nearly full. Galileo realized this occurs because Venus is closer to the Sun than the Earth is. We see different areas of Venus lit because the angle between the Sun, Venus, and the Earth changes.

Telescopes also showed that thick clouds always surround Venus. The clouds block us from seeing Venus's surface. In the 1700s and 1800s, better telescopes were built. In the 1900s, giant telescopes were built. Still, none could see through Venus's clouds.

Mariner 10 photograph of Venus taken from a distance of 450,000 miles

WAS VENUS EARTH'S TWIN?

Astronomers like to solve mysteries. They try to figure out what Venus is like even though they cannot see its surface.

The astronomers know that Venus has much in common with the Earth. Venus is 7,520 miles in diameter. The Earth is a little bigger. Venus's year is the closest in length to the Earth's. And Venus is

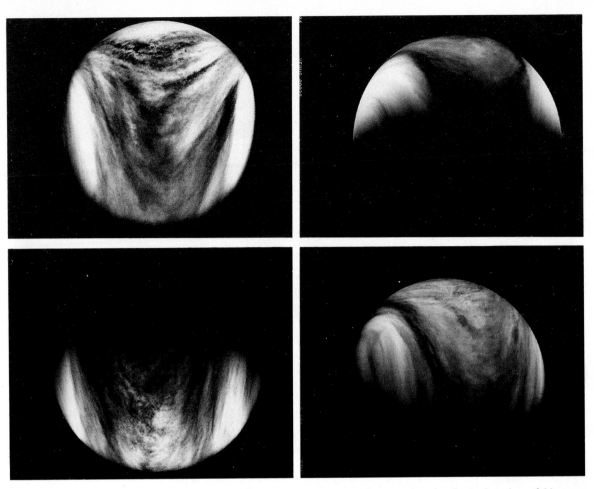

The *Pioneer-Venus* spacecraft sent back photographs of Venus.

the nearest planet to the Earth. Because of all they have in common, Venus was nicknamed "Earth's Twin."

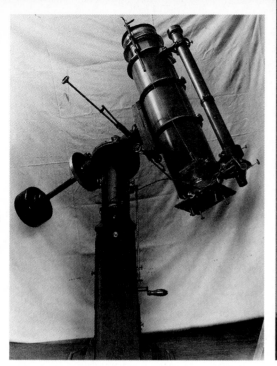 

A six-inch telescope (above) used at Yekes Observatory in Wisconsin about 1900. The two-hundred inch Hale telescope (right) at the Palomar Observatory in California was built in 1948.

By the early 1900s, some astronomers thought Venus might be like Earth in other ways. They thought it might have air. They figured Venus might be a little warmer than

Earth. And they thought its clouds might produce rain.

Several astronomers decided that Venus was similar to the Earth millions of years ago. Venus had swamps beneath its clouds, they said. They thought dinosaurs and other reptiles might live on Venus.

This 1,000 foot curved dish in Arecibo, Puerto Rico is the world's largest telescope. It was used to study Venus in the 1970s.

During the 1960s, astronomers discovered a big difference between Earth and Venus. The Earth takes 24 hours to spin once. That means a day on the Earth is 24 hours long. Working with *radar* (a tool that uses radio waves to make out the shape of things), scientists found that Venus spins once every 243 Earth-days. So a day on Venus is 243 Earth-days long.

Venus differs from the Earth in many ways, but that was not learned until rockets were sent to Venus.

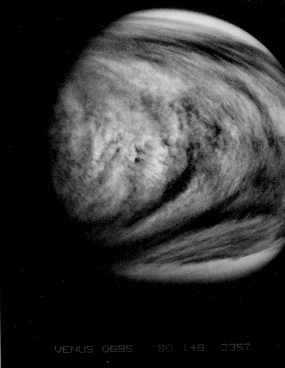

VENUS 0695   80 149   2357

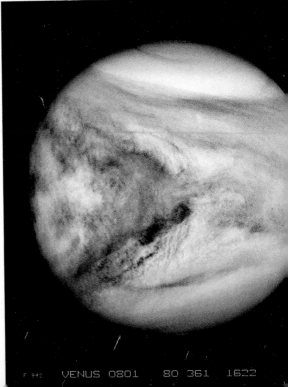

F 942   VENUS 0801   80 361   1622

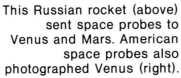

This Russian rocket (above)
sent space probes to
Venus and Mars. American
space probes also
photographed Venus (right).

ROCKETS REACH VENUS

The space age began in
the late 1950s. Soon after
that, both the United
States and Russia began
launching *space probes* to
Venus. Space probes carry
cameras and instruments
but no people. They send
pictures and data back to
the Earth. Between 1961
and the 1980s, Russia and
the United States launched
more than 20 space

Drawing shows the path *Mariner 10* will take to explore Venus and Mercury.

probes toward Venus. In
only a few years, the
probes provided more
information about Venus
than had been learned in
all earlier history.

The probes found that
Venus is not "Earth's Twin"
at all. In fact, Venus has
some of the harshest
conditions in the Solar
System.

First, Venus lacks
oxygen. And its clouds do
not contain water drops.

They are made of
substances that would
poison us.

Venus also is very hot.
The hottest temperature
recorded on Earth was
136° F. The temperature on
Venus is about 850° F.
No water exists on
Venus because the heat
would boil it away. Venus's
surface may have puddles
of glowing red metal.

Although Venus seems
to be lifeless, it has

Using the information sent back by space probes, an artist painted this picture of Venus.

interesting scenery. It has flat regions called *plains*. It has canyons and valleys. And Venus has huge mountain systems. Venus's highest known peak is called Maxwell Montes.

Paintings of the active volcanoes (above) and Maxwell Montes (below)

About six miles tall, Maxwell Montes is a little higher than the Earth's tallest peak, Mt. Everest.

Data from the probes showed that several of Venus's mountains may be active volcanoes. Radar studies made from the Earth in the late 1980s showed that Venus's volcanoes may have erupted in recent years.

WHAT HAPPENED TO VENUS?

Astronomers were surprised by what the probes revealed about Venus. The planet is hotter and more unfriendly toward life than had been thought. Since Venus is the closest planet to the Earth, many astronomers had expected it to be more like our planet.

What happened to make Venus so different? Some

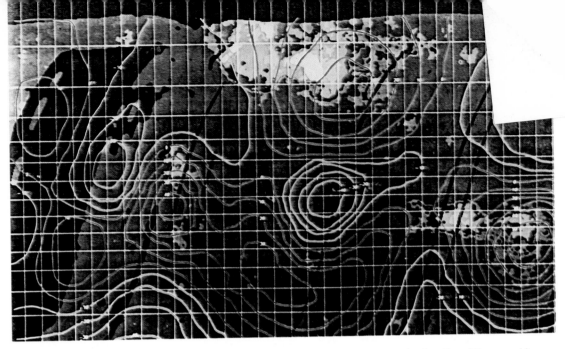

This chart shows the gravity measurements of Venus made by the *Pioneer Venus* spacecraft. The lowest level of gravity shows up in yellow.

scientists think that Venus
and the Earth were alike
long ago. Venus may have
had oceans. Perhaps it
had an atmosphere much
like the Earth's long ago.
Venus could have had
living things.

DR. THOMAS A. SWIFT ELEMENTARY SCHOOL
SCHOOL DISTRICT No. 34 (ABBOTSFORD)

Events on Venus may have sent it down a different path than the Earth. The "Greenhouse Effect" may have played a big role on Venus. A greenhouse lets in heat, but keeps most of it from escaping. As a result, a greenhouse is warm. By letting heat in but blocking its escape, Venus's clouds may have turned the planet into a giant greenhouse. That could be the reason Venus is so hot

Greenhouses are built to allow light in and to trap heat inside.

and has no oceans today.

That could be a lesson for us. Planets naturally change over billions of years. The Earth has changed in many ways during its five billion years. For example, the

Once Earth looked like this.

dinosaurs have come and gone.
And the climate has changed
many times.

   We, human beings, are

newcomers to the Earth.

We have been around only
two million years—a short
time in the Earth's life. But
in the last one hundred
years, we have greatly

Humans, and the machines they build, are polluting the Earth's atmosphere.

changed the Earth's air. We have made it very dirty. This air pollution seems to be causing a "Greenhouse Effect." The lesson learned from Venus is: If we don't clean up our air, the Earth

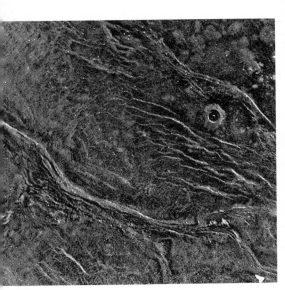

Russia's *Venera*
spacecraft (right)
made this radar
image (above) of Venus.

could become too warm
for human beings.

Astronomers still have
many questions about
Venus. Did Venus have
oceans? If so, why did
they disappear? Why did

Venus heat up? Does
Venus have fossils of
plants and animals that
lived there when the
planet was more like the
Earth? Can we learn more
about how the Solar
System was formed by
studying Venus?

Other space probes will
be sent to Venus. One day
astronauts may even
explore Venus to help
solve the mysteries about
the planet. The answers
could do more than just

teach us about the second
planet from the Sun. It
could teach us to take
better care of the third
planet from the Sun—our
Earth.

FACTS ABOUT VENUS

Average Distance from Sun—67¼ million miles

Closest Approach to Earth—25 million miles

Diameter—7,520 miles

Length of Day—243 Earth-days

Length of Year—225 Earth-days (Venus's year is shorter than its day)

Temperature—About 850° F. on Venus's surface

Atmosphere—Mainly carbon dioxide, with lesser amounts of nitrogen and some other gases

Number of Moons—0

Weight of an Object on Venus That Would Weigh 100 Pounds on Earth—89 pounds

Average Speed as Venus Orbits the Sun—About 22 miles per second

WORDS YOU SHOULD KNOW

ancient(AIN • shint)—very old

astronauts(AST • roh • nawts)—space explorers

astronomers(ah • STRON • ih • merz)—people who study stars, planets, and other heavenly bodies

atmosphere(AT • muss • feer)—the gases surrounding some heavenly bodies

billion(BILL • yun)—a thousand million (1,000,000,000)

fossils(FAW • silz)—very old remains of plants and animals

Greenhouse Effect(GREEN • house eh • FEKT)—a condition in which heat is let in but kept from escaping

Maxwell Montes(MAX • well MON • tez)—the highest known peak on Venus

moons(MOONZ)—natural objects that orbit seven of the nine planets

orbit(OR • bit)—the path an object takes when it moves around another object

oxygen(OX • ih • jin) — a gas we need to breathe

phases(FAYZES) — changes in the amount that a planet or moon is lit up by the Sun

plains(PLAYNZ) — large, nearly flat pieces of land

planets(PLAN • its) — large objects that orbit stars; the Sun has nine planets

pollution(puh • LOO • shun) — the dirtying of the Earth's air, water and land

radar(RAY • dahr) — a device that finds objects by bouncing radio waves off them

Solar System(SO • ler SIS • tim) — the Sun and its "family" of objects

space probes(SPAISS PROHBZ) — unmanned spacecraft sent to study heavenly bodies

stars(STAHRZ) — giant balls of hot, glowing gas

Sun(SUHN) — the yellow star that is the closest star to the Earth

telescopes(TEL • ih • skohpz) — instruments that make distant objects look closer

universe(YOO • nih • verse) — all of space and everything in it

Venus(VEE • nis) — the second planet from the Sun

volcano(vawl • KAY • no) — an opening in the ground through which lava and other material erupt; a mountain, also called a volcano, builds up around the opening

INDEX

About the Author

Dennis Fradin attended Northwestern University on a partial creative scholarship and was graduated in 1967. His previous books include the Young People's Stories of Our States series for Childrens Press, and Bad Luck Tony for Prentice-Hall. In the True book series Dennis has written about astronomy, farming, comets, archaeology, movies, space colonies, the space lab, explorers, and pioneers. He is married and the father of three children.

DR. THOMAS A. SWIFT ELEMENTARY SCHOOL
SCHOOL DISTRICT No. 34 (ABBOTSFORD)

DR. THOMAS A. SWIFT ELEMENTARY SCHOOL
SCHOOL DISTRICT No. 34 (ABBOTSFORD)